SEASONS OF SALVATION

A WEEKLY DEVOTIONAL
50 WEEKS

MAE McKNIGHT

Copyright 2015
By
Mae McKnight

ISBN 978-1-940609-38-6
Soft cover

All rights reserved
No part of this book may be reproduced or transmitted in any form or by any means, electronic or mechanical, including photocopying, recording, or by any information storage and retrieval system, without permission in writing from the copyright owner.

Bible translations from KJV, NIV, AMP

This book was printed in the United States of America.

To order additional copies of this book contact:

Hissheep1948@msn.com
Or
Amazon.com

FWB

SEASONS of SALVATION

Learning	**SPRING**	We Are Re-Born
Casting Roots Down	"Budding"	Fresh yet Fragile
Teaching	**SUMMER**	We are Growing
Spreading Roots Out	"Blooming"	Shining in the *Son*
Guiding	**AUTUMN**	We Are Changing
Stronger Roots	"Colors Fading"	Plowing The Soil
Listening	**WINTER**	We Are Helping
Deeper Roots		Patiently Preparing

"Planting and Protecting"
Next Spring's Seeds
Witnessing… Waiting… Watching…

FOR HIM!

"And they overcame him by the blood of the Lamb, and the word of their testimony" Revelation 12:11 KJV

TABLE OF CONTENTS

DEDICATION 11
FOREWARD.. 12
ACKNOWLEDGEMENTS 13
INTRODUCTION... 15
AUTHORS NOTE 17

PART ONE – SALVATION

WEEK ONE.. 20
MY SALVATION
The Pastors Visit

WEEK TWO 23
GROWTH AND GOSSIP
Don't Misunderstand

WEEK THREE 31
LOVE
Judgement

WEEK FOUR 35
BEWARE! STOP! COMMIT!
Saved Lord, What Does That Mean…?

WEEK FIVE 40
TODAY IS THE DAY!
Questions and Answers

WEEK SIX 43
WHISPER THE NAME
I Yield Again

WEEK SEVEN 46
IT'S A WALK
Stop and Look Up

WEEK EIGHT 50
    LAY IT ALL DOWN...FOR GOOD
        Just Trust Him
WEEK NINE 53
    HIS CHILDREN... A LETTER TO GOD

PART TWO: TRIALS AND FEARS

WEEK TEN... 62
        TRIALS
        Be Prepared
WEEK ELEVEN.. 66
        SEEK HIM FIRST
        Calm Down!
WEEK TWELVE 71
        I AM STILL HERE
        Come Quickly
WEEK THIRTEEN... 74
    I AM WELL IN JESUS' NAME
        I'm Afraid... Again
WEEK FOURTEEN... 78
        DARKNESS TO LIGHT
WEEK FIFTEEN... 80
        JESUS IS THE HEALER
        Jesus Is My Healer
WEEK SIXTEEN... 83
        GLORIFY THE LORD
WEEK SEVENTEEN... 86
        SADNESS
        Sadness to Sorry

WEEK EIGHTEEN	89
JUST IMAGINE	
The Sun is Just a Cloud Away...	
WEEK NINETEEN...	92
YOU KNOW THE REAL ME	
God Knows My Heart	
WEEK TWENTY..	95
USELESS FEAR	
Fear	
WEEK TWENTY-ON...E...	99
PICK ME UP LORD	
Day One	
WEEK TWENTY-TWO...	102
HOPE AND REST IN HIM	
I'm Tired	
WEEK TWENTY-THREE..	105
VALLEYS	
The Sun Isn't Shining...	
WEEK TWENTY-FOUR..	109
THOUGHTS	
Be Thankful For Trials	
WEEK TWENTY-FIVE..	113
WHAT MONEY?	
Father, You Are Wise	
WEEK TWENTY-SIX..	117
I AM BLESSED	
Bible Reading	
WEEK TWENTY-SEVEN...	121
TRUE TREASURES	
Restore My Heart Anew	

WEEK TWENTY-EIGHT.. 124
WHERE NOW LORD?
WEEK TWENTY-NINE.. 127
YOU ARE PATIENT, LORD
Always – You First
WEEK THIRTY.. 130
NOW IT'S MORNING
All in a Day's Work
WEEK THIRTY-ONE... 133
FAITH & HOPE
Discouragement Dawns
WEEK THIRTY-TWO... 136
MY REPENTANT HEART
The Gift
WEEK THIRTY-THREE.. 139
SEEK THE GIVER
Christ, The Key

PART THREE: VICTORY AND ENCOURAGEMENT

WEEK THIRTY-FOUR..149
SIGNS OF THE TIMES
The Joy of The Lord is Our Strength
WEEK THIRTY-FIVE..153
THE LAST VICTORY
Free at Last
WEEK THIRTY-SIX...157
LORD, I CAN'T WALK BY MYSELF
We Never Are Apart

WEEK THIRTY-SEVEN	160

   LORD, I NEED YOUR HELP
    Trying is Tiring

WEEK THIRTY-EIGHT	165

   GIFTS & TRIALS
    Your Gifts & My Trials

WEEK THIRTY-NINE	170

   THE PROMISE
    Sitting At Your Feet

WEEK FORTY	174

   MY BENDED KNEES
    My Constant Comfort

WEEK FORTY-ONE	178

   OUR WITNESS
    He's Always Near

WEEK FORTY-TWO	182

   A SERVANT'S HEART
    May I Help?

WEEK FORTY-THREE	185

   MY TESTIMONY
    Trusting In Him

WEEK FORTY-FOUR	188

   DAY BY DAY
    Not By My Might

WEEK FORTY-FIVE	192

   NO REST, NO PEACE… ALONE
    Full Circle

WEEK FORTY-SIX	195

   MY FRIEND… GOD'S SERVANT

WEEK FORTY-SEVEN..198
MY HEART
Help Me Hear You
WEEK FORTY-EIGHT..202
IT'S ABOUT HIM... NOT ME
Fear of the Enemy
WEEK FORTY-NINE... 208
THE SONG & THE DREAM
WEEK FIFTY...211
DEUTERONOMY 30:19

DEDICATION

This book is dedicated to my parents, Lloyd and Leona Lindsey.

They moved us to a farm when I was three years old.

We always had lots of family; some even lived with us, and were always welcome.

Farm life is a hard life and my parents worked long hours to provide for us.

We were poor and I make no apologies for being honest. The fact is we didn't even know that we were, because so many families were.

We always had plenty to eat, a nice warm bed to sleep in and a house full of family who always loved us.

We were taught to love one another, and always respect our elders.

We were taught how to work and take pride in our chores.

My three older brothers, Wayne, Jim, and Dale were blessed with me the first-born girl in 1948.

Our Mom was not well and no one ever expected we would be blessed with my only sister, Sharon.

Down through the years God has surely blessed our family. Our parents have gone to be with Jesus, but all my siblings and I, are still enjoying life watching our children and grandchildren learn and grow.

My prayer is that we will all be together through eternity with Jesus!

FOREWORD

I have known Mae for several years and have found her heart to be one after God's own heart. Her desire is to see the Body of Christ walk with hope and encouragement in their everyday life.

I believe she has found a way to do this through her writings in "Seasons of Salvation". Through the Word of God as well as her thoughts and inspiration through the Holy Spirit, Mae offers words of Hope, Encouragement and Victory in Christ.

I would encourage all to use this book as a weekly devotional to give you what you need to walk in the Power of God's Word.

The blank pages at the end of each section can be used to record your own thoughts and hopes for the future and even perhaps, help in writing your own book.

We all have "Seasons" in life, some good and some difficult. But God offers the answers to every situation through His Word. Mae has captured some of these answers and offers them to you with her book, "Seasons of Salvation".

Pastor Lois A. Hoshor

ACKNOWLEDGEMENTS

I would like to thank everyone who will open both heart and mind, as pages are turned and words are read.

You will notice the usage of both KJV and NIV translations.

Simply pray, open *your* Bible, and hear God's voice.

Please don't miss the message because of the messenger.

In the final steps of getting the dream of this book from my heart and mind – into this book that I hold in my hand – I sincerely say:

Special thanks to my friends and family; you have laughed with me and cried with me on this part of my journey. You, like me, truly believe God will use whom He chooses to do His will in His time! Eternity with Jesus awaits! Praise His name!

Morgan LeMay is a thirteen year old, seventh grader. She attends Vinton County Middle School, where she is currently taking college classes with the CCP (College Credit Plus) program. She enjoys reading, sketching, listening to music, and watching crime dramas. She is a Girl Scout and she is on her school volleyball team. She hopes to play tennis in high school and become a veterinarian or an artist. Morgan has a loving family and has attended Zaleski FWB Church since she was one week old.

Thank you Morgan. Who would have imagined that God would send you, a thirteen year old, to accomplish this goal? He always knew! I look forward to more books together. Always walk with Jesus and obey Him, as He guides your steps.

Thank you, Dr. Alton Loveless. Since our first meeting nine years ago, you have been kind, understanding, and patient. Because of you, all the writings God has given to me will be shared in print to help others in their 'Seasons of Salvation.'

Finally, to my husband David, I know that your Saturday OSU football games have been interrupted, your meals have been late (or not at all) if I was in the middle of a thought process. You have endured computers, papers, pens and Bibles on tables and floors, as I sorted through, checking and double checking. Thank you for preparing meals for me, doing my chores, driving me around, and patiently waiting. Most of all, thank you for praying for me and my family. We love you! Thank you for sharing your family with me. I have been welcomed and loved always. For bringing my morning coffee and breakfast, and at the end of so many long days, covering me with a nice, warm blanket, watching me fall asleep in peace and safety. Thank you... I love you!

"He brought me to the banqueting house, and his banner over me was love." Songs of Solomon 2:4 KJV

INTRODUCTION

Forty years of writing and waiting have now come to pass!

"To everything there is a season, and a time to every purpose under heaven…" Read Ecclesiastes *3:1-8 KJV*

I share with you some of the "seasons" in my journey.
I have traveled with God, turned my back on God,
I have run back to Him… when I came to myself.
He put my "Jesus" ring on my finger so I would remember.
He called me His Bride in 1997. Read *Luke 15:11-32*

Unlike a *daily* devotional, you now have an entire week.
Don't hurry!
You have two weeks off for a guilt free vacation!
Seek God, hear, obey, and record on the note pages what you've learned.
Allow Him to write His love on the tablets of your heart.

Remember: *your* own day of "salvation".
How did *your* family and friends re-act when they heard the **Good News**?
What were *your* "trials and fears"?
Did *you* doubt- More than once?
What questions did *you* have?
How did God lead *you* through to *your* "victory and encouragement"?

I'm still on my journey… How about you?

If you have not begun your journey with God, start today!

...Now is the accepted time... now is the day of salvation.
II Corinthians 6:2

AUTHOR'S NOTE

I LOVE THE BIBLE- GOD'S HOLY WORD.

He knows my very best intentions. My desire is to read, study, and pray more.
But, I admit that I need structure and discipline to get, and keep myself on track.

It's too easy to get busy with my day. Soon the time is gone, along with another opportunity... again!
At days end, feeling guilty, and sad, I promise to do better tomorrow.

A great help for me was, my e-mail "daily devotional". Surely this would help.
But, I found myself hurrying to my computer each morning, (most of the time) before the phone rang... I would click and read. Mission accomplished! One day as I was driving, It occurred to me that I had no idea what I had read that morning!

Had I only justified rushing through my time with God?
The sadness and guilt were back.
I realized time was still dictating and I was only cheating myself by trying to hurry.
I'm ashamed to admit that sometimes I have read many days at one sitting if I were behind!

NOW THAT IS GUILT!

Self-imposed for sure. God wants to communicate with us. He doesn't care what the calendar or the clock says. All our days, and time belong to Him!

That is why designating an entire week, instead of a day for each study will allow you to relax and take the time you need to explore the Scripture noted. Pray and ask God to reveal His path for your life as each day passes. You have so much to offer!
Allow Him to use you to declare His glory! It's never too late, He is always on time!

If you have found yourself in this situation, give yourself a pat on the back...
You're learning. Give yourself a break, and don't be so harsh and judgmental.
Put a smile on your face and joy in your heart because Jesus Lives and God Loves you!

Be of Good Cheer,

Mae McKnight

SALVATION

WEEK ONE

MY SALVATION

It was quite a phenomenon that year. It was 1974.

In the small, Southeastern, Ohio City, people were talking!

Things were happening!

The excitement had spread to the small surrounding villages too.

In our little village, population 700, the children were excited!

They were helping each other learn Bible verses.

They were wearing little red and white beanies on their heads.

They couldn't wait to board the church bus on Sunday morning!

The strangest thing was that mothers and fathers were riding those busses with their kids!

What was the buzz?

It was a new pastor in an old church; fresh anointing on the "flock", and a new "flock" too.

People were going to church, who normally never would have.

They were also inviting friends and neighbors.

That's how it happened.

My friend, Ruth, came to my house one morning, inviting me to bring Darci, Angi, and Gary, my three kids, and join her and her two daughters, Julie and Amy, on Sunday morning. She was my best friend. How could I say no?

Plus the kids were all excited about going on the bus.

They were town kids and they walked to school, but now... the bus!!!

I had been raised in church. I knew about God. We even prayed during meals and before bedtime.

Now, our lives were full of sports, band, Blue Birds, and lots of other school things.

I thought that I was doing all the right things, but I had not done the one thing that was "most important", get saved!

Well, we went that Sunday and the church was packed! I saw a lot of people I had gone to school with; some I hadn't seen in years. On the back seat in front of me, were little prayer cards. They were for attendance and prayer requests. I read it carefully. Reluctantly, I checked the tiny box, requesting a visit from the pastor.

This is what happened next...

THE PASTOR'S VISIT

Take away the sin and shame,
Take away the strife.
Cleanse our heart, O Master,
Give us eternal life.

Into our home the pastor came,
He came to talk to me
About my soul and love for God,
And life eternally.

I knew I was a sinner
When I let him in that day,
And I was surely tempted
To just look at him and say

"I'm sorry but I changed my mind
This life will never do,
For I can never live it,
I'm not strong in faith, like you."

My heart was pounding loudly,
And I thought I couldn't breathe.
Oh why did I invite him here?
Oh why can't he just leave?

But as I sat and talked to him
On that hot summer day,
I was truly sorry for my sins,
I knew that *they* must go away.

He showed me in the Bible
Four things that I must do
To really know that I am saved,
And give my life to You.

Repent, Believe, Confess, Receive,
I did these things that day.
Now I'm so glad that the pastor came,
I'm glad that he *did* stay!

Oh Lord, You saw me yielded there
And sorry for my sins,
And though I wasn't worthy,
Your salvation entered in.

May I bring honor to Your name
In things I do and say,
For the power in Your precious Blood
I thank You, Jesus, everyday!

Written for Pastor John Maxwell, Faith Memorial Church, Lancaster, Ohio 1974

WEEK TWO

GROWTH AND GOSSIP

The church grew and grew. People were getting saved and baptized. Lives were being changed! We became the fastest growing Sunday school in the state of Ohio. Families were coming and staying.

As always when showers of blessings are falling, Satan, our enemy, must come against us... and he did.

Soon, we heard grumbling from unbelievers and disgruntled Christians from other churches.

Next, it spread inward to the part of the congregation, who forgot, or never really knew, it was not all about them!

Psalm 109:1-5 NIV

"O God, whom I praise,
Do not remain silent,
For wicked and deceitful men
Have opened their mouths against me;
They have spoken against me with lying tongues.
With words of hatred, they surround me;
They attack me without cause.
In return for my friendship they accuse me,
But I am a man of prayer.
They repay me evil for good
And hatred for my friendship."
Father, help us keep our eyes on You. Amen

DON'T MISUNDERSTAND

"Our pastor is so busy",
You hear it everywhere.
Why, he's been so busy lately
That he forgot to care.

About the souls that are coming in,
Every single week.
He walked right by ME Sunday, and
He didn't even speak!

I just stood back and waited
As he walked on through the door
He's so used to seeing ME that
He doesn't care anymore!

He's overpaid and has the most
And best of everything.
It must be nice, not to work…
No, not do anything!

A preachers' job is easy.
Anyone can say a prayer.
And all I hear are numbers,
When I go to church out there!

He wants you saved, then when you are,
He moves on to someone new,
He completely stops caring
If *you* follow through.

Well……..
Yes, our pastor's busy,
This I don't deny.
If I may take a moment,
I'll try and tell you why.

First, you say there's numbers,
You hear them, that's for sure.
Each of them a "lamb of God"
Walking through the door.

When you hear the numbers,
Instead of getting mad,
Think about all those souls,
And let your heart be glad!

You say he's rich and it's not fair,
He doesn't do a thing.
Anyone can say a prayer,
And stand and talk and sing.

No matter what material wealth
We have upon this Earth,
The only thing to profit us
Is a spiritual re-birth!

A man that's chosen out by God
To preach and spread the Word,
Is always a ready target,
The vision's often blurred.

You think his job is easy?
Why don't you ask his wife?
In the many hours she spends alone,
She sees the other side.

The phone is always ringing,
Meetings always to attend,
Shut-in friends are waiting,
A marriage there to mend,

A funeral or a wedding.
Both sadness and joy.
"Will you come and pray with us
For our little boy?"

"Please talk to God and help us",
People plead with him each day.
Only those in touch with God,
Can really, truly pray.

You say he wants to get you saved,
Then doesn't care if you stray.
My friend, he cares, but even Jesus,
Preached to thousands and walked away.

The fields are white with harvest,
So many to bring in,
He can help you find the road to home,
But *you*, must stay faithful to the end

WEEK THREE

LOVE

Judge not lest you be judged...
You will be judged by the same measure by which you judge...
Unreal expectations of others and ourselves...

Why do we make it so hard on ourselves and others to just be happy in the joy of the Lord?
Have you ever heard of the "Golden Rule"?
Read Jesus' message to us is *Matthew 7:12*.
Love one another and treat others the same way we want to be treated by them.
Time hasn't changed that. Love and kindness are so important.
A simple smile will still break the ice from around the coldest heart.
We can't distinguish between a cold heart and a wounded heart, but God sees the heart of each of us and He knows our ways.
Father, search my heart and clean me up so that my prayers for others are not hindered. Amen

JUDGEMENT

I had a person say to me
Just the other day,
"A lot of people come to church,
But how many of them stay?"

Well I've often thought about that
And I've even wondered too,
What can a person do or say
To help another through?

You say a lot are saved out there
But few still look the part.
Well, would you like to tell me,
Have you seen inside their heart?

You can't judge, nor can I
That belongs to God.
You aren't walking in their shoes,
As down the road of life they trod.

They still have ups and downs, like you,
And temptations every day.
You don't hear them every time,
They turn to God and pray.

Don't be fast to condemn the ones
Who walk out and down the aisle.
You may see "hurry" on their face,
But in their heart's a smile.

WEEK FOUR

BEWARE! STOP! COMMIT!

There isn't anyone who hasn't been torn in thought by Satan.
In our daily struggles, it's so easy to put on the "poor meezies", and mop our brow in despair.
Next, usually comes something like, why me?
I try really hard; I don't do a lot of bad things like *that* person does.
Look at all he has! Look at how God blesses him!
Beware!
You are headed down a rat hole.
The rat who is leading you is your enemy!
Stop!
Commit yourself to God.
Resist the devil and he will flee from you. He has no choice!
Read the sovereign Word of God, *James 4:7*.
Look inward, ask for guidance, and ask for forgiveness.
Start praising! Lift your hands and heart in Thanksgiving!
Humble your self and The Mighty God will lift you up. Read *James 4:6*.
"Flee the evil desires of youth, and pursue righteousness, faith, love, and peace, along with those who call on the Lord out of a pure heart", 2 Timothy 2:22 NIV
Dear Father, help us to be honest first with You, then ourselves, as well as with others. Read *1 Peter 2:1*... Help us grow up! Amen.

SAVED LORD, WHAT DOES THIS MEAN...

How can this all be?
This great salvation in Your Word
You speak with great authority.
Because You died so we could live.
What greater gift
Can we give?
Oh Jesus Christ on Calvary
Why did they nail You to a tree?
Why did You, God, let Him die?
Did You hide Your face to cry?
Did You say, this should not have been
Or did You say this is the end?
These things Lord, I often do.
I mumble and pout about what's fair, but
Now, Oh Lord, I see You there,
With outstretched hands, Oh Lord I see
You are saying, Lord to me...
Saved Mae, how can you be?
You grumble and complain and pout
If things don't go your way.
You don't consider others' problems,
As you deal with them each day.
You are so quick Mae to condemn,
To find a fault, to hold it in.
You say to you, "I've done my best,
Lord, I'm better than the rest."
But You Lord say, this cannot be...
You are no better, Mae to me.

You are My child, but many more
Are calling on My name.
Then I must fall upon my face,
And I must take the blame!
A mystery of Your love, Dear Lord
You have shown to me.
I did not know I felt that way
As I did bend my knees to pray.
Jesus Christ you saw it there
Contempt inside of me.
Envy, strife and jealousy
Self-pity most of all.
Now, it's coming clearer,
I've risen for the fall!
I must get closer, my Dear Lord,
My heart is crying out,
Then Satan says, "You sure you're saved?"
And then, I start to doubt.
Dear Lord, nail me to that tree
And let the tear drops flow
So I may dwell Oh Lord with Thee
Let You hear Lord, LESS of me.
Let me be Lord, first a friend
Give me a loving heart,
Not just for the ones I love
Rather, let me start...
Let me see me as others do and,
Pick myself apart!
Then Dear Jesus, I will say

Saved… Oh Lord, this can be.
Thank You for another day
Another lesson You have shown
My heart's so full of love
My God still lives, I know He's there
In Heaven, up above.

WEEK FIVE

TODAY IS THE DAY!

We all have our point of no return!
Where will we be? When will it be?
What does it take?
What is the last straw that will break the camel's back?
Or the sinner's heart... you know what I mean.
We've all been there, resisting, rebelling and procrastinating.
We were hoping against hope we would always have tomorrow.
Now is the accepted time of salvation. Read *II Corinthians 6:2*
God is merciful, it is not His desire that anyone should perish.
He wants us all to come to repentance. Read *II Peter 3:9.*
When will we realize we can't make it alone?
We were not designed to be self- sufficient. We are created beings!
"So God created man in his own image, in the image of God he created him; male and female He created them." Genesis 1:27. KJV
What an honor to praise and worship our Lord and Savior, Jesus.
He is worthy!
Father, help us to come sooner than later. We don't want to miss any of Your blessings! Amen.

QUESTIONS AND ANSWERS!

What does it take to make someone?
Be sorry for his sin?
What does it mean when Jesus saves?
And salvation enters in?
Why is man so full of doubt?
He tries to have his way?
And why does our Dear Lord
Forgive us, each and every day?

Because he sent His Blessed Son
To a world so dark and gray
To teach us many lessons
All things old must pass away.

Our home tho nice upon this Earth
We all must leave someday
Now I'm building a mansion,
With my Savior I will stay.

WEEK SIX

WHISPER THE NAME

Stop and just whisper the awesome name of Jesus.
Name above all names!
Tension, stress and worry... none of those can remain in the presence of the sweetest name ever heard... Jesus.
Try it while driving or in any stressful situation.
Just whisper and repeat, Jesus... Jesus... Jesus...
You will experience His peace. There is something so humbling... yet so uplifting when you call upon the name of our Master and King.
 We are not slaves, we have free choice to serve and worship.
Read *Romans 6:22*.
"I wait for You, O Lord; You will answer O Lord my God."
Psalm 38:15 NIV
"I will instruct you and teach you in the way you should go; I will counsel you and watch over you."
Psalm 32:8 NIV

Dear Father, thank you for Your peace. No one can steal it from me and I refuse to give it away. Amen

I YIELD AGAIN

You always call me to my knees
When I won't hear Your voice.
You won't make me stop and pray
You've given me free choice.

Help me hear Your voice today
Just as clearly as can be
And bring me to my knees again
For a closer walk with Thee.

You've shown me again today
That You do answer prayer.
Because I knelt and prayed to You,
You saw me yielded there.

With a plea for help and guidance
And an emptiness of heart,
You took me to Your Holy Word
And filled the empty part.

WEEK SEVEN

IT'S A WALK

When I was first saved, my mind was like a sponge.
Just like a sponge, it got overloaded and soggy when I didn't rest.
God expects us to use wisdom in everything.
We can push ourselves too long and become frustrated.
Sometimes the challenge for me is to just be still and stop analyzing.

"Be still and know that I am God; I will be exulted to the heathen and in the earth." Psalm 46:10 KJV
It isn't about learning the whole Bible in a year, even if you could. You can read the whole Bible in a year, but how much will you remember? How much will become rhema to your heart?
It's a walk...
Sometimes a power walk through The Book of Acts...
Sometimes a slow meandering through The Book of Psalms...
Sometimes simple reflection and just sweet peace.

"But seek Ye first the Kingdom of God and His righteousness; then all these things shall be added unto you." Matthew 6:33 KJV

Dear Father, help us to relax, and take time to enjoy our daily walk with you. Amen

STOP AND LOOK UP

Why can't I learn, Oh why can't I?
What's standing in my way?
Confusion or pressure
The stressors of the day?

I can't let anything interfere
With learning about my Dear Lord!
I cannot forget one single word
It's a price I cannot afford!

What holds me back?
Why can't I dig deep?
Although I'm awake,
My mind is asleep!

I'm trying so hard,
Can that be it?
Am I trying too hard
To make pieces fit?

My mind is a blank
Oh what can it be?
What lesson Lord
Are you trying to teach me?

Must I come in the morning
When the new day is fresh and
Facts can stay in my mind?
What can it be Lord, please help,
The answer tonight I must find!

*Yes, your mind's tired
Now you need rest
In the morning
You'll be at your best.*

*Please put Me first
Don't put Me last,
Love Me, My child more and more,
Draw closer tomorrow
Than you did today,
See the blessings I have in store!*

Thank You Lord! You are so good to me!

WEEK EIGHT

LAY IT ALL DOWN... FOR GOOD

Many times I have been my own worst enemy.

I've always been an average person, a B or C, a few A's sprinkled in, here or there. That has never been quite good enough to please me. Many burdens I've carried for too many miles, trying to do my best. The truth was... I already had!

I had achieved my B+, but I was still carrying the guilt, shame, and hurt, because I felt like a failure. How could I just quit?

When I finally laid it all at the foot of the cross, I got an A+ for effort and a huge lesson in humility!

God did not expect me to carry all this on my back, it was too heavy and I couldn't stand. He did expect me to do what Jesus said, *"Take My yoke upon you, and learn of Me; for I am meek and lowly in heart; and you shall find rest for your souls; For my yoke is easy and My burden is light." Matthew 11:29-30 KJV*

Dear Father, help us to leave the sins and burdens at the foot of the cross, never to drag them back to us again. Thank You for mercy and grace. Help us to hear the final grade, well done good and faithful servant. Read *Matthew 25:23*. Amen

JUST TRUST HIM

Lord, why can't I ever be
The Christian You expect of me?
Why can't I ever stand the test?
Why am I weaker than the rest?
I know I'm saved, but Lord, how long
Will it take me to get as strong
As other Christians that I see?
Please pour Your Spirit out on me.
As days do come and quickly go
Send Your Spirit, Lord to show
Me how to walk down life's road
With an easier and lighter load.
Just knowing that you answer prayer
And for Your children You do care
Because You died on Calvary
So all Your people could be free.
Not just a few... No, You said all
You will hear us when we call
Upon Your Name in earnestness
And put our aching hearts at rest.

WEEK NINE

HIS CHILDREN ... A LETTER TO GOD

We all have our story, they are all different, yet very much the same. When we truly listen to those around us, we find that we are all searching for love, hope, peace, joy and acceptance.

We want to be safe, respected and cared for. We want to believe our lives are important and that our living has made a positive impact on at least one other person.

We hope someone will miss seeing us and hearing our voice, when we are gone from this earth.

They may even smile when they remember our smile or our silly little laugh, which sounds more like a five year old than a fifty year old!
A tear or two may be shed... but not too many... and not for too long... because... We have gone to be with Him... Hallelujah!

"Beloved now we are the sons of God, and it does not yet appear what we shall be: but we know that, when He shall appear, we shall be like Him; for we shall see Him as He is."
I John 3:2 KJV

The world of sin, is broad and deep,
Much as the pit of Hell,
Many redeemed Christians
Have a great story to tell!

Dear Lord,

    I've often tried to pray, the words will not come to me. Do I try too hard to say the right things? Precious Heavenly Father, look down on me now I pray. I know that truly, I am not worthy of Your love, Dear Jesus. Why do You put up with me? How can I grow stronger, in love for other people?

    I feel ashamed of my hurting heart. Take away this hurting tongue and most of all, my pride! Take it all and empty me of anything that does not reflect a loving heart. Help me to be a friend to all those who want me for their friend. Help me to love those who do not love me. I need help to endure hurt feelings and patience too. Help me be master over my temper and just be filled with Your peace, joy and love. I'm sorry... Thank You.

    I'm asking these things Heavenly Father, through the Precious Blood of Your Son, Jesus, in honesty of heart. I believe you have heard me and have answered my prayer for HELP! Not in my time, but in Your time, which is perfect. In Jesus Name I pray... Amen.

Love,
Mae

TRIALS & FEARS

WEEK TEN

TRIALS

In this world we will have tribulation, temptation and doubt.

Hearing the Master's voice is all important.

How can we hear if we don't listen?

Jesus said, "'*My sheep hear My voice, and I know them, and they follow Me.*'" John 10:27 KJV

"The sheep that are My Own hear and are listening to My voice; and I know them and they follow Me." John 10:27 AMP

He warns of danger and reassures us of our safety and salvation.

Dear Father, Help us to be sensitive to your voice and run from the temptations and run to Eternal life with you! Amen

BE PREPARED

Today Satan came again
And knocked upon my door.
The knock was even louder
Than it's ever been before.

These days have been impossible
I've hardly time to breathe
From the pressure that I feel on me,
I feel like I could leave.

But, Oh Dear Lord, where would I go?
I could never just walk out
And leave my family and my home,
There isn't any doubt.

You saved me Lord from my sin
Through Your precious Blood
And I can feel the Glory,
Of that precious Cleansing Flood.

You warned me Lord, ahead of time
You told me it would come
So I would not be unprepared
Until the battle's won!

I'm calling on Your Name, Dear God,
Temptation is so great
To scream and lose my temper
But I know it's not too late.

Forgive me Lord, of all my sins
And help me start anew,
Give me strength to solve my problems,
And keep my eyes on You!

WEEK ELEVEN

SEEK HIM FIRST

Taking time to seek God's will is so important in our daily lives.
We would never think of spending twenty – four hours a day,
Seven days a week with a friend or loved one in silence…

We would surely be talking to them and listening to them speak to us.
We might ask for their in-put on the smallest matters, such as, "What would you suggest for dinner?" We are so interested in their opinion, when that is truly all it is…

How much more should we seek God's instruction and guidance?
How many times do we forget to give the day over to Him early?
"But seek first His kingdom and His righteousness, and all these things will be given unto you as well." Matthew 6:33 NIV.

He is with us 24/7, and he has all the correct answers!
"As for God, His way is perfect; the Word of the Lord is flawless."
Psalm 18:30 NIV
"It is God who arms me with strength and makes my way perfect."
Psalm 18:32 NIV

Dear Father, help us to remember to give the day over to you ...

Help me to take my hands off so that You can guide me in Your perfect way. Amen

CALM DOWN!

Temper is confusion
Confusion leads to doubt
Envy, strife and jealousy
We need to kick these out!

Thoughtlessness and whining
Self-pity that's for sure
An hour in The Word each day,
Surely is the cure.

For Christians who believe The Word
Can still get pulled away
By all these things
Plus neglect in time we take to pray.

I don't have time, I'll wait awhile
My work is piled sky high
If someone comes and sees this mess,
I know that I'll just die!

How foolish can a person be?
It's not others we should please.
If first we'd pray and read The Word
Our minds would be at ease.

In complete communication
With The Father and The Son,
While walking in The Spirit
Our work will soon be done.

What a brighter outlook
The gloom is washed away
It pays to always keep in touch,
The Lord may come TODAY!

You are so good to me, praise God!

WEEK TWELVE

I AM STILL HERE

When our days are so long and all seem to run together, it's hard to just STOP! We just keep on going and trying to figure out a plan... one <u>everyone</u> can live with. Trying to please everyone usually pleases no one!

We become frazzled and worn at which point we are of no use to anyone...
Except God ...when we come to the end of ourselves, then He can use us.

Who knows why we wait so long? We end up saying something brilliant such as, "Well, I don't know what to do but just pray!" I wonder if God laughs, cries or just shakes His head and says," Here we go again, when will they learn?"
We know that He waits patiently again... until we 'humble down.'
He isn't interested in flowery words and phrases. This is definitely not the time to try to impress Him when we know we can't anyway. Get real!

He is interested in getting us back in a right relationship with Him, so He can help. When we just come as a sad and tired child in need of our Father, then He picks us up and renews and refreshes us, as only He is able.

"Therefore, whoever humbles himself like this child is the greatest in the kingdom of heaven." Matthew 18:4 NIV

COME QUICKLY

Call upon My name My child
For your soul I still care
And I will not forget you
Nor, will I leave you there,

Underneath the circumstance
Where sin and death you meet
Bring your burdens straight to Me
Just lay them at My feet.

This trial is almost over
The sun is shining thru
Don't forget to stop and pray,
My promises review.

For I am still the same, My child
It's your life that has changed
So when your day seems much too long
Just call upon My name.

I will bring you peace and rest
To end a long, long day
In My power, I'll hold you fast
So your faith won't go astray.

WEEK THIRTEEN

I AM WELL IN JESUS' NAME

Sometimes when we hear of sickness in others, that fear tries to attach itself to us; for example...
Your friends'... friends'... neighbor has just been diagnosed with an inoperable brain tumor. Now suddenly, you have all the symptoms!

I know that sounds far-fetched but, remember... Satan is a liar!
He gives us just enough truth to make his lies believable!

Is it possible you have just developed a brain tumor in the past few minutes of the phone conversation? Is it probable?

After all you do have a headache that has lasted a few days... Hmmmm...

The fear of sickness and death can be paralyzing to a perfectly healthy person. Stop the downward spiral which is bound to follow if you continue in the fear! Speak the Word, which says, *"For God hath not given us the spirit of fear; but of power and of love, and of a sound mind."*
II Timothy 1:7 KJV

Then confirm and take your stand with this:
"I will not die but live, and proclaim what the Lord has done."
Psalm 118:17 NIV

"Thou wilt keep him in perfect peace, whose mind is stayed on Thee: because he trusteth in Thee." Isaiah 26:3 KJV

Dear Lord, thank You for my health... mentally, physically, emotionally and spiritually. <u>Then, pray a specific prayer for the person who really does have the illness, don't worry if you don't know their name... God does.</u>
Thank you for Your healing power. Amen

I'M AFRAID... AGAIN

Rid my troubled heart of fear
Let me know that You are near.
Because You said Lord, You would be
Walking with me endlessly.

As I go to bed tonight
Let me hold Your hand so tight.
Rid my thoughts of earthly woe
So always Master, I will know
I'm not alone and left in fear,
Because Dear Jesus, You are near.

Today I learned a whole new thing,
The joy in praying for others brings.
Today the Lord taught me to pray
In a new and special sort of way.
In mighty greatness He has shown,
When we know Him, we're not alone.

WEEK FOURTEEN

DARKNESS TO LIGHT

Dear Lord I feel deserted
On some dark, distant shore.
I was not satisfied with You,
I searched and searched for more.

My friends all had it, but did I?
I never felt that way.
What I would give, if I just had,
That much of You today.

- Always remember that Satan is a liar!
- His goal was to get my eyes on man.
- God had not left me, He promised!
- Don't fall into self-pity.
- Call upon the Name above all names, Jesus.

"Wherefore God also hath highly exalted him and given him a name which is above every name." Philippians 2:9 KJV
"That at the name of Jesus every knee should bow, of things in Heaven, and things in earth, and things under the earth;" Philippians 2:10 KJV
"And that every tongue should confess that Jesus Christ is Lord, to the glory of God the Father." Philippians 2:11 KJV

WEEK FIFTEEN

JESUS IS THE HEALER

Oh Lord, when I am weak... you are strong!
All four of the Gospels... Matthew, Mark, Luke and John are full of the healing miracles which Jesus performed while He was here on this earth.

He told the disciples they would even do greater works than He!
Read *John 14:12*
Wow! My mind can't comprehend the sights they witnessed with Jesus in their midst. What a healing Savior! Jesus was able to heal everywhere He went when the people had faith and believed. Even Jesus was amazed at the lack of faith in His home town. He could not do any miracles there, except lay hands on a <u>few sick people</u> and heal them. Read *Mark 6:5-6*

My eyes have witnessed miracle healings, twice they have been my own.

Mostly though, I have seen and been healed more slowly. He reminds me to take care of my body that is the key. He expects us to use wisdom and apply the knowledge we have. Of course we must trust and believe that He is more than able to heal and make us whole... fast or slow... here or there... Jesus is the Healer.

Dear Father thank You for Your healing power thru the blood of Jesus. Amen

JESUS IS MY HEALER

When my health is not so great, and
I don't feel so well,
Remind me of the place
You've prepared for me to dwell.

Oh Lord, I know I'm weak
In body, soul and mind
It's hard to reach that joy, and
Peace is hard to find.

So Heavenly Father
In Jesus name, just now I pray,
Touch me with your healing hand...
Close beside me stay.

WEEK SIXTEEN

GLORIFY THE LORD

Help me use Your gifts, Dear Lord
To glorify Your name.
Don't let our hearts be boastful
In search of wealth or fame.

For what we have and what we are
We owe it all to You,
Tomorrow with the morning light
Your mercies will be new.

"This I recall to my mind, therefore have I hope. It is of the Lord's mercies that we are not consumed, because His compassions fail not. They are new every morning: great is Thy faithfulness." Lamentations 3:21-23 KJV

Gifts are such a controversial subject with many Christians. God gave us many gifts we do all agree on...
The breath in our body, our five senses... sight, hearing, taste, touch and smell; our mind with reasoning and our heart with the ability to love.

Best of all, the greatest gift... His only Son Jesus who died to save us.

"For God so loved the world, that He gave His only begotten Son, that whosoever believeth in Him, should not perish, but have everlasting life." John 3:16 KJV

Heavenly Father, help us to remember to bless You always for all the gifts that come straight from You. We are nobody with nothing without You. Amen.

WEEK SEVENTEEN

SADNESS

This is the first poem that I wrote when I did not call on the Lord for help and guidance.

I didn't even notice for ten years this was the turning point.

I did just what I said I would never do… I let Satan have his way!

I got so mad at God and I could not believe He would abandon us.

My life was a disaster and I dragged on and on and on…

I didn't think there was any hope.

Now I wonder why I didn't read my own poems.

God was speaking to me; I wouldn't listen!

I was just too angry, to full of bitterness and pain.

Forgive me Father.

"I am weary with my groaning; all the night make I my bed to swim; I water my couch with my tears. Mine eye is consumed because of grief; it waxed old because of all mine enemies." Psalm 6:6, 7 KJV

SADNESS TO SORRY

Why are you so cast down
Oh my foolish heart?
Satan rules this world
Your home is not set apart.

Where once my heart did laugh
When love and trust I had
My heart is breaking now,
My eyes can see, but sad.

Trust and love are precious things
My heart is breaking now
I have my share of heartaches,
More I won't allow.

This was a decisive point in my walk with The Lord.
Looking back now, twenty-three years later, I know!
My hurt was so deep; I looked within instead of looking up!
I rejoice in His forgiveness and love!

"Blessed is He, whose transgression is forgiven, whose sin is covered." Psalm 32:1 KJV

WEEK EIGHTEEN

JUST IMAGINE

I love clouds. They have always fascinated me, the way they move across the sky. I especially love the big puffy ones. They are the ones going nowhere, but are everywhere people take the time to look up and really see them.

Children lie on the ground on the hot summer days and use their imagination as they visualize monsters, animals, and big scary lakes with fog.

The same clouds may be viewed by young lovers who see castles and ocean beaches. Through the years I have imagined everything I suppose at one time or another. But now I see rows and rows of sheep led by the Great One in front...

He knows the way... Of course... He is the way!
I am most inspired when the sun's streaks of light shoot down from behind the dark clouds. It always makes me smile, and reminds me that God is still there, even in gloomy times.
He smiles on us and showers us with His blessings.
  Dear Father, who are we to have been given the honor to view and enjoy Your creation? Thank You, we praise You. Amen.

Who has the wisdom to count the clouds? Who can tip over the water jars of the heavens? Job 38:37 NIV

THE SUN IS JUST A CLOUD AWAY...

I see it peeking thru
The sky so cloudy round about
Is keeping it from view.

Sometimes our life upon this earth
Appears to be this way, and
We are almost certain,
That the clouds are here to stay.

If we let this get us down
We'll never see the sun
Our very lives will fade away
Our days on earth are done.

But in the hope of our Dear Lord
If we will keep the faith
He will never leave us
For by His redeeming grace,

We are saved and sanctified
Our future's in His hands
The cloudy days that hide the sun,
Are part of God's perfect plans.

WEEK NINETEEN

YOU KNOW THE REAL ME

God knows our heart. He knows everything about us. He knows what we are thinking and feeling, even when we are so hurt and sad, we stop feeling.
He knows ...
We may resist calling on Him or just ignore the gentle tugging of His Spirit calling us to pray and talk to Him... He still knows... He's God!
Everywhere... all the time...knowing all... seeing all... that's who He is!

How happy and relieved He must be when we finally get humble, get real, and truly communicate with Him. He is not waiting patiently to condemn us and make us feel guilt and shame.

No! Rather, He is waiting patiently to take those feelings away from us.
He won't take away anything unless we ask, but when we do, He rescues us with haste. That's His great pleasure, to give us the gift of forgiveness.

"Fear not little flock; for it is your Father's good pleasure to give you the kingdom." Luke 12:32 KJV

Thank You Heavenly Father for Your loving kindness and restoration.
Thank You for Your Word which reminds us that, there is none perfect, and assures us that, *"If we confess our sins, He is faithful and just to forgive us our sins and to cleanse us from all unrighteousness." I John 1:9 KJV*

Help us to remember Satan is the accuser and he wants us to remain down and out.

We can't see the Son shine while looking at the ground.
"But thou, O Lord, art a shield for me; my glory, and the lifter up of mine head." Psalm 3:3 KJV

GOD KNOWS OUR HEART
With peace and love our heart does fill
When once we've taught our heart to still.
Not a trouble, nor a fear
When the blessed Savior's near.
God in Heaven knows us best
Our heart with Him can be at rest.

He holds our hand and pulls us through
'cause He loves me and He loves you.
So when our heart is full of strife
And we are troubled in this life,
We can always kneel in prayer
And know our blessed Savior's there.
He isn't there to say we're wrong
To knock us down, where we belong...
To earthly size and aching heart
We shall never be apart
He is always waiting there,
He knows our heart and hears our prayer.

WEEK TWENTY

USELESS FEAR

Fear takes many shapes...sickness is probably the biggest stumbling block for me. My Mother was in poor health and near death many times while I was very young. I cried at school because I wanted to be home with her.

Satan used that same fear against me for fifty – seven years! It never truly was revealed to me until this year when she went to be with the Lord.

All those years I worried and she lived to the age of eighty-seven!

This year, my own illness has been a major deterrent to my joyful dance of praise. When you don't feel well whether it be body, mind or spirit, it's more difficult to be joyful and peaceful. The older we get the more aches and pains are present too.

But...
The older we get in the Lord... the more able we are to recognize the tricks of the Enemy. He wants to steal our joy and leave us powerless.

Remember, he quotes Scripture too.

He was even bold enough to quote the Word to Jesus, *"The devil led Him to Jerusalem and had Him stand on the highest point of the temple. 'If You are the Son of God,' he*

said, 'throw Yourself down from here.' <u>For it is written</u>,' He will command His angels concerning You to guard You carefully; they will lift You up, in their hands, so that You will not strike Your foot against a stone." Luke 4:9-11 NIV

Satan knows: "...the joy of the Lord is your strength." Nehemiah 8:10 KJV

FEAR

Our burdens seems so heavy here.
So often we can't see
An end to this rough, rocky road,
There must surely be.
I love You Lord, and trust You too this always is my plea-
Gracious, Heavenly Father,
Is there something wrong with me?
I worry so about my heart
As each new day goes by,
Why am I so afraid,
Am I afraid to die?
Oh Lord, I know that You do live
And You alone do know
The reason I was put on earth
A few short years ago.
I'm praying for more strength again
My God this is my plea,
Please grant it Lord
Just now I pray,
A closer walk with Thee.

WEEK TWENTY-ONE

PICK ME UP LORD

Moving to a strange area and leaving all familiar aspects of our life can be very difficult and unnerving, no matter what your age.

Attending a new school can be terrifying too, especially if it is the middle of the year. When you walk into the class room for the first time, you just feel piercing eyes that are burning a hole through your body!

Starting a new job is one of the scariest things I've ever done. You have new challenges both mental and physical. Sometimes needing to get up earlier than your normal time can put such stress on you that it's impossible to get to sleep at all! You may be as I was, just back into the work force after many years at home with the children.
Maybe you found yourself saying what I did... Help!
I am so thankful to have the Lord, my God, Jehovah Nissi..."
The Banner" that goes before me. He makes straight my path and gives me strength to carry on.
Father, Your Word says, the battle belongs to You. Help us look to You and trust in You at all times. Amen.

"This is what the Lord says to you: 'Do not be afraid or discouraged because of this vast army; for the battle is not yours, but God's....'" II Chronicles 20:15 NIV

DAY ONE

The hour is late
It's dark outside, but I am wide awake.
Thinking of my brand new job,
My knees begin to quake.

Can I do the work they expect?
Will I even fit in there?
I need this job, I want this job,
So this is now my prayer.

Lord help me to get well quick
Standing straight and strong
I need a lift of Spirit, Lord
In my heart a brand new song.

Well, an old song, not a new one
One I've sung before
The love and hope of Jesus,
He's knocking at my door.

I've been alone and I can't stand
I've fallen by the way
Please pick me up and help me Lord,
As You did the other day.

WEEK TWENTY-TWO

HOPE AND REST IN HIM

When I'm tired many times the days are just too long and too full.
After struggling to see the fruits of this day, which seem to elude me?
I wonder where it is all going, and who cares anyway?

Just like the Teacher, son of David, King of Jerusalem, wrote in the
Book of Ecclesiastes..."*what does man gain from all his labor?*"
"*...everything is meaningless.*" Read *Ecclesiastes 1:2-3 NIV*

But, after twelve chapters, King Solomon ends by saying:
"*Now all has been heard, here is the conclusion of the matter:*
Fear God and keep His Commandments,
For this is the whole duty of man." *Ecclesiastes 12:13 NIV*

Dear Father, when we become frustrated with life and the endless string of *seemingly*, thankless tasks and errands we must complete, we must sound ungrateful for all Your provisions. Help us to remember happiness is only found when we have found You and dedicate our lives to Your service.
"*Everything you do, do it unto the Lord, with thanksgiving*".
Amen.

I'M TIRED

I'm tired Dear Lord,
I need the guidance of Your hand,
The comfort of Your Word, a reassuring
Statement telling me,
From sin, I'm free.
How You sent Your precious Son,
To save a wretch like me.
Oh God of countless wonders,
In amazement I do dwell,
As I read and learn the story,
That the Holy Bible tells.
A thoughtless human though I am,
You still have time for me.
And even though my body's tired
My eyes at last can see.
The Savior of great blessings
With knowledge men do speak,
But oh, to share Your Kingdom, Lord,
This blessing I do seek.

WEEK TWENTY-THREE

VALLEYS

When I was a little girl, my Grandmother lived with us. She was blind, but she had "perfect sight." We shared her big bed and at night she would always tell me stories as I fell asleep. Often, one story just left me wide awake and ready for another, but she never seemed to mind.

She told me lots of Bible stories and the Twenty-Third Psalm. I loved to hear stories of David, the shepherd boy and his sheep. Being a farm girl, I under-stood sheep. I would imagine myself watching over the sheep and writing songs to God.

I loved to hear the Twenty- Third Psalm, but the part about *"The valley of the shadow of death",* always scared *me* to death!!! In fact, I was so scared; I didn't even hear the part about... *"I will fear no evil."*

I'd cuddle up to Grammy more closely when she was coming to that part. She didn't mind, she loved me.

My wonderful Grandmother left this earth many years ago. She had to leave me, she had no choice He called her to be with Him. Her many years of waiting to be with her Jesus finally arrived. I know we will meet again.

As I've grown older, the rest of the Psalm has become my reassurance...

"For Thou art with me." All through my life when I'm too tired, too anxious or too scared to pray...I just cuddle up a little closer to the Lord, where I'm safe. He doesn't mind... he loves me! HE will Never leave me... Never!

Read *Psalm 23*

"Be strong and courageous. Do not be afraid or terrified because of them; for the Lord your God goes with you; he will never leave you or forsake you." Deuteronomy 31:6 NIV

THE SUN ISN'T SHINING...

The sky's dark and gray
It's not bubbling joy that I feel,
But a sense of belonging
And deep earnest peace,
That makes my salvation so real.

The valleys are deep
And sometimes so dark
I can scarcely see any light
High upon the mountaintop,
The sun is shining bright.

Thank God for a Savior we can trust
Thank God for a Bible we can believe
Thank God for His saving power and grace,
For eternal life we can receive!

WEEK TWENTY-FOUR

THOUGHTS

I'm so comforted to know that God does not expect us to be perfect!
Actually, he expects us to admit that fact and lean solely on Him.
"For all have sinned, and come short of the glory of God; being justified freely by his grace through the redemption that is in Christ Jesus." Romans 3:23-24 KJV

There is none perfect, no not one!

Only One was tempted and tried and did not sin. He is the Perfect Lamb of God... He of course is Jesus, God's only Son, our Lord and Savior.
He stood firm as our example. Read *Luke 4.*

Will we stop sinning on this earth? NO! But, we will NOT stop asking His forgiveness and moving on... the Apostle Paul said,
"I press toward the mark for the prize of the high calling of God in Christ Jesus." Philippians 3:14 KJV

"He is the Rock, his works are perfect, and all his ways are just. A faithful God who does no wrong, upright and just is He." Deuteronomy 32:4 NIV

"It is God who arms me with strength and makes my way perfect." II Samuel 22:33 NIV

Dear Father, Thank you for your mercy and grace. Help us to grow up along the way so we may be an example of Your kindness and love. Amen.

BE THANKFUL FOR TRIALS

A person's thoughts aren't always
Joy and peace and love,
But we follow our instructions
From the good Lord up above.

Sometimes thoughts are heavy
Our carnal self creeps in,
How can we thank God for the trials?
If the battles we can't win?

Lord, we aren't perfect
We are only flesh and blood.
You saw us there, just sinners
In the murky mire and mud.

When we fall short, You still forgive
If we are sorry for our sin,
You'll lift us up, so we can start...
Our Christian walk again.

WEEK TWENTY-FIVE

WHAT MONEY?

One of the biggest complaints I have heard my whole life is, church, preachers and money! If you doubt this watch the expressions change at the mere mention of the word… offering!

Unfortunately we all have heard the stories of funds being mismanaged or handled improperly at best. Why would the "church" be any different?
Satan has his greedy hand everywhere he can. What better place to attack than Christians? He hates all of us, but he especially hates God's servants.
Since they live in a "fish bowl"… the "world" has an easy view.

Dear Father, help us use wisdom through prayer and divine direction, being good stewards of the money you bless our lives with. Remind us not to judge because you see all. We can use our time more wisely. Amen.

"For God will bring every deed into judgment, including every hidden thing, whether it is good or evil." Ecclesiastes 12:14 NIV

"Remember this: whosoever sows sparingly will also reap sparingly, and whosoever sows generously, shall reap generously. Each man should give what he has decided in

his heart to give, not reluctantly or under compulsion, for God loves a cheerful giver. And God is able to make all grace abound to you, so that in all things at all times, having all that you need, you will abound in every good work." II Corinthians 9:6-8 NIV

FATHER, YOU ARE WISE

As the Spirit leads you
The minister did say
But Lord, I just can't believe
Things should be done this way.
Your Spirit was with us Lord,
I felt Him oh, so near
I pray that You won't leave us
While this confusion now You hear.
A place so sweet and holy
A meeting in Your name
Bless us now Dear Savior
Has this turned into a game?
I don't want to think that this is wrong
I know I can't judge
Just erase this bitterness,
Don't let me hold a grudge!
Get behind me Satan
Get those thoughts away
And rid my mind of all these doubts,
Forgive me, now I pray.

WEEK TWENTY-SIX

I AM BLESSED

Since God created everything, I believe He wants us to enjoy the work of His hands. To have the freedom to read and study my Bible wherever I want, is a privilege and honor. I do not take this blessing lightly.

Nearly ten years ago, God impressed on my heart to pray for His children around the world, who are not blessed with freedoms as we are.

He reminded me how many are tortured and killed for their faith and love for Him. Night after night as I began to pray, I would begin to cry and intercede for them. I wondered... would I be so courageous and strong?

I can study the Word on my patio in the bright summer sun or enjoy the fragrance of spring flowers, or the brilliant colors of falling leaves. I can watch the snowflakes fall quietly, as I wait in my car, reading my Bible...

Redeeming precious time. Though I pray so, this may not always be true.

Father, forgive us for being so careless with our time and our freedom.

Help us remember and pray earnestly for all those who have and will lose their life for Your name's sake.

Help us never to forget that to die while in Your service is gain. Amen.

"Preach the word; be prepared in season and out of season; correct, rebuke, and encourage - with great patience and careful instruction."   II Timothy 4:2 NIV

"Remember Jesus Christ, raised from the dead, descended from David. This is my gospel, for which I am suffering even to the point of being chained like a criminal. But God's word is not chained. Therefore I endure everything for the sake of the elect that they too may obtain the salvation that is in Christ Jesus, with eternal glory." II Timothy 2:8-10 NIV

BIBLE READING

To lay a good foundation
When studying the Word
Then putting into action
The principles I've heard.

Sometimes the learning's slower
And it takes lots of time
Sometimes I get discouraged,
It's like an uphill climb.

To get things in perspective
Can sometimes go so slow
To read it once and then again
And find I STILL don't know!

Because my mind was drifting
Jam packed with other things
From the frosty snows of winter,
To the butterflies of spring.

Dear Lord, forgive my laziness
Help me now to use my mind,
Not just to read, but to retain
Redeeming precious time.

WEEK TWENTY-SEVEN

TRUE TREASURES

Thankfulness, a thankful heart, and tears of joy...
they all go together at my house.
When I think of all the blessings, the Lord has showered upon me
It is just too awesome to imagine!
We live in a cottage, not a mansion, and something always needs repaired or replaced. Who knows... maybe that's the same way it is in castles and mansions too; just more things, more often.

My treasures have changed as I have. I've replaced my diamonds for my Jesus ring. I know someone will always have a bigger diamond... a brighter stone.
But, no one will ever have a stronger Savior; He's the "Chief Corner Stone!"
He's my Rock, my Foundation, and my Friend; what more do I need?
Father, thank you for your blessings and a new mind set of priorities. Amen.

"Consequently, you are no longer foreigners and aliens, but fellow citizens with God's people and members of God's household, built on the foundation of the apostles and prophets, with Christ himself as the chief cornerstone. In him the whole building is joined together and rises to become a holy temple in the Lord. And in him, you too are being built together to become a dwelling in which God lives by his Spirit." Ephesians 2:19-22 NIV

RESTORE MY HEART ANEW

This week has been so busy Lord,
What did I do for You?
Did I bring glory to Your Name?
Did I remember You?

I've had some time to think about
This week that just went by,
Remembering how You've cared for us,
I feel that I could cry.

For all these lessons I have learned
And all the things You've shown
This week in my brand-new life,
I KNOW that I have grown!

You've blessed us with so much Dear Lord,
My heart's so full within
That when I try to cut this short,
I just begin again...

So all I'll say is thank You God
What more is there to do?
Praise and glory to Your Name,
Restore my soul anew.

Tomorrow starts a whole new week
With each demanding day
Please walk beside me step by step
Close beside me stay.

WEEK TWENTY-EIGHT

WHERE NOW, LORD?

A quiet sense of peacefulness
A love so deep inside
In times of absent mindedness,
Please, Holy Spirit, guide...

Us to that place that's set for us
A perfect place of peace
With the noise around about us
Our haven, our release.

It's easy Lord, to come and go
Leaving family far behind
Not for selfishness I say,
I need a quiet mind.

Church three times a week
Reading Bible in between
Neglect of my family, you say?
But I really haven't been.

To witness for the Lord is great, and
We can't be ashamed
Always ready with an answer,
Oh praise His Holy Name.

So I'll do this, and I'll do that
I'll run to and fro
I'll be there, if I'm late,
It's so important that I go.

Many people build a church
But from home, we too can pray
I think I see The Message,
Sometimes... it's more important if I stay.

As parents, we must be sensitive to the needs of our children.
God has given us an awesome responsibility.
We must use wisdom and much prayer.
Seek His face to see where you belong and when.
When we are obedient, He will be glorified.

"...choose you this day whom ye will serve ...but as for me and my house, we will serve the Lord." Joshua 24:15 KJV

WEEK TWENTY-NINE

YOU ARE PATIENT, LORD

When we get so busy everywhere...with everything...sometimes...   We just need to STOP!
When I become too busy to spend time with the Lord... that's too busy.
I just need to get my mind off me and on Him.

You don't know about a person unless you spend intimate, quality time with them. It's Your name Lord; I should keep on my lips and in my mind.

The Psalmist David knew about keeping God first. He wrote:
Psalm 8:1 "Oh Lord, our Lord, how excellent is Thy name in all the earth!
   Who hast set Thy glory above the heavens."
Psalm 9:1 "I will praise Thee, O Lord, with all my heart;
   I will shew forth all Thy marvelous works."
Psalm 9:2 "I will be glad and rejoice in Thee:
   I will sing praise to Thy name,
   O Thou Most High." KJV

Dear Heavenly Father, forgive me for being too busy for You.
Thank You for **never** being too busy for me. Amen.

ALWAYS – YOU FIRST

A new sense of awareness
Crept into my heart today.
The blessed presence of The Lord,
A love I can't repay.

I have been so busy
Trying to figure what was wrong
All wrapped up inside myself,
I forgot where I belong.

Oh Lord, the beauty of the earth
My eyes cannot behold
Patiently waiting... still for me,
Your wonders to unfold.

WEEK THIRTY

NOW IT'S MORNING

Morning is such an important time for us. It sets the stage for the entire day.
Maybe that's why mornings are so hectic. Our enemy, Satan, knows how to get us upset, make us late, and worry. He certainly does not want us to put on the "full armor of God", as Paul warns us in *Ephesians 6;* otherwise, we will extinguish all the flaming arrows he sends our way!
He wants us to go away from the Lord, early, and then we are more vulnerable to his attacks!

There we are sitting ducks on the sea of hurry, fret, worry, and anxiety.
We are now an easy target for Satan, he is a master marksman; he knows our weakest points.
We can just as easily be protected and safe, we have a choice!

Dear Lord, Your Word says, *"In the morning, O Lord, You hear my voice; in the morning I lay my requests before You and wait in expectation." Psalm 5:3 NIV*

Search my heart Lord, take out any unclean thing and make my ways acceptable to You. Amen.

ALL IN A DAYS WORK

Now it's morning, did you pray?
Will you work for Him today?
The way we live is our own choice
But listen to your Master's voice.
Let me be willing when You call
To crown You, Jesus, Lord of all!

Oh God, what can I say?
What can I ever do?
To even halfway show You, Lord,
How much that I love You?
Search my heart, just now I pray
And help me grow to be
A more effective witness,
Dear Jesus Christ for Thee.

WEEK THIRTY-ONE

FAITH AND HOPE

Faith and hope... what would we be without them?
Without them, I'd just sit down in a heap in the corner.
What a horrible conclusion if this world is all there is...
As beautiful as God has made His creation, there's more...

We certainly don't live in a worry free, stress free, or crime free world.
But, we have hope, that there is a better one in our future, where our stay will be longer... forever. We have faith in the One who told us this is true.

"Let us fix our eyes on Jesus, the author and perfecter of our faith, who for the joy set before him, endured the cross, scorning it's shame, and sat down at the right hand of the throne of God." Hebrews 12:2 NIV

"And hope does not disappoint us, because God has poured out his love in our hearts by the Holy Spirit, whom he has given us." Romans 5:5 NIV

Dear Lord, help us never to lose hope in your coming and faith as the saints who have gone before. Amen

"Therefore since we are surrounded by such a great cloud of witnesses, let us throw off everything that hinders and the sin that so easily entangles, and let us run with perseverance the race marked out for us." Hebrews 12:1 NIV

DISCOURAGEMENT DAWNS

As I live and breathe, Dear Lord
Will I remember You?
Can I remember all the times
Your love has pulled me through?

A constant keen awareness
Telling me to calm and pray,
But I've defied that tenderness,
Now, has it slipped away?

A gentle tugging at my heart
A memory now and then
A flash of Jesus through my mind,
I hear Your voice again.

I have truly found You
I know this love is sure
So in the hours of this day,
My faith and hope restore.

WEEK THIRTY-TWO

MY REPENTANT HEART

Sometimes it seems all I get done is repenting. Am I always that neglectful, I ask? Just when I feel like everything is going great and my walk is stronger than ever before… my impatience shows and my temper flairs! Just when more than anything, I want to stay calm and peaceful… there comes that temper again! After I calm down, I wonder… was that me? When will I learn to use tolerance for the intolerable people, I ask? After all, I AM ONE!

I relate to Apostle Paul, when he said: *"For in my inner being I delight in God's law; But I see another law at work in the members of my body, waging war against the law of my mind, making me prisoner of the law of sin at work within my members. What a wretched man I am! Who will rescue me from this body of death? Thanks be to God- through Jesus Christ our Lord! So then, I myself in my mind am a slave to God's law, but in the sinful nature a slave to the law of sin."* Romans 7:22-25 NIV
If Paul was in a dilemma… how can we not be also?
Don't you just love the way Paul starts out in Chapter 8? He does not leave us hanging … *Verse 1." Therefore, there is no condemnation for those who are in Christ Jesus"* 2. *"Because through Christ Jesus the law of the Spirit of life sets me free from the law of sin and death."*

Dear Father, You never leave us hanging either. You just wait for our repentant heart and heal all the places we ask You with our repentant words.
Thank You. Amen.

THE GIFT

Dear Lord, I've been neglectful
In my reading and my prayer.
You have heard and answered me,
You've shown me You still care.

Tomorrow I'll do better
I'll start the day out right
Be with me and guide my steps,
I pray I won't lose sight...

Of You and yes, eternal life
You've promised, it is free,
A gift that I do not deserve,
A sinner such as me.

You've been with me, I know Your love
As endless days have gone
Keep us safe and free from harm,
Until You bring us home.

WEEK THIRTY-THREE

SEEK THE GIVER

So many churches have split and so many wonderful, God-fearing people have been wounded to the point of "forsaking the assembling together"
With their brothers and sisters in Christ. Why?

There are lots of disagreements concerning the spiritual gifts.
- Are they for today?
- Is there a prayer language?
- Are tongues simply languages of other nations?
- Can people really get healed today?
- How about prophesy and interpretation?

"But the fruit of the Spirit is love, joy, peace, patience, kindness, goodness, gentleness and self-control. Since we live by the Spirit, let us keep in step with the Spirit. Let us not become conceited, provoking and envying one another." Galatians 5:22, 23, 25, 26 NIV

Paul was no stranger to the feuding and disagreements, that is why he said, *'Therefore, my dear friends, as you have always obeyed- not only in my presence, but how much more in my absence-continue to work out your own salvation with fear and trembling, for it is God who works in you to will and to act according to his good purpose.'" Philippians 2:12-13 NIV*
Dear Lord, how we must grieve You to see the anger and the quarrelling by Your people toward one another. Forgive us Lord and fill us with Your love. Amen.

CHRIST, THE KEY

Not the gift, but The Giver
That's the key.
Christ is the One who set us free.

So, when for gifts you do thirst,
Be sure to seek The Giver first.

Spiritual feelings are really great,
On this, some people meditate.

The Word of God has lasted long,
Old time Christians, can't all be wrong.

They love The Lord with all their heart,
They've read all The Word, not just part.

God knows what gifts to give to who,
I can't say what's right for you.

The gift that I will seek,
Is to watch my tongue, when I speak.

VICTORY & ENCOURAGEMENT

WEEK THIRTY-FOUR

SIGNS OF THE TIMES

In October 1975 I wrote this poem.
In 2002 my granddaughter shared it with her class at the Christian Academy.
Everything was still relevant, only more so.

Now, in 2015, we must fight for all our religious freedoms.
So far we fight by our vote, but who knows what another thirty years will bring?
If not for Christ in us the hope of glory, would you want to be here at all?
Our country in every facet of government needs our prayers.
Our parents, siblings, children and grandchildren need our prayers.
Our friends and neighbors need our prayers... the list goes on...
Praying is a full time job. There is no place to stop!

Oh Dear Lord, humble is what we hear. Forgive us pride and arrogant attitudes.
Have mercy on us, and on our land. Please God, bless America again. Amen.

"If my people which are called by my name, shall humble themselves and pray and seek my face and turn from their wicked ways; then will I hear from heaven and will forgive their sin and heal their land." II Chronicles 7:14 KJV

THE JOY OF THE LORD IS OUR STRENGTH

To face a world of crime and sin
It's impossible without God.
To hear of bloody war
On the ground where Jesus trod.

The Bible is in the newspaper
You'll find this on any page.
To point this out to a sinner
Will surely set him in rage.

Many laws are being made
Against freedom toward our Lord.
Our prayers are being censored
It's a price we cannot afford!

The days seem dark and dreary,
We are tempted just to quit.
When we see how far our money goes,
Nothing seems to fit!

The many things of evil
Are tempting in the world.
Now someone has wronged you,
Another dirty dig you've hurled.

Yes, the situation of the earth
Looks very bad indeed.
Sin and shame, my friend,
Are growing like a weed.

Just to know that my Lord lives
Surely gives me strength
For putting joy back in my day,
My heart is filled with thanks.

WEEK THIRTY-FIVE

THE LAST VICTORY

In the twenty-first century man can do anything.
He can make it…buy it… borrow it…and of course some simply steal what they want; some things don't change with time.
Money seems to buy everything, and for much of our lives, we are at least content with little or no thought toward eternity.
Who can even fathom eternity? If it were possible, perhaps we would be a little more cautious about the way we chose to spend our days here on earth.

No, with all the knowledge… all the wisdom… and all the money and gold known to man, God is still in total control of our death and it's time.
You may say," That isn't true, people commit suicide every day." True.

However, how many more people *attempt* to end their days, and by all the laws of nature and science, it should be accomplished. Still, they are spared from their own physical destruction.

God will not be mocked, He is still the Creator of heaven and earth, the Alpha and the Omega, the First and the Last, and He will have the last word!

"Do not be deceived: God is not mocked" Galatians 6:7 KJV

"Show me, O Lord, my life's end and the number of my days;
Let me know how fleeting is my life." Psalm 39:4 NIV

Dear Father, thank You for taking away the fear of death in our lives. As surely as the flowers fade and die, so shall we. But, grace be to You, Lord.
You have overcome hell, death and the grave, Amen.
Read: I Corinthians; 15:53-54-55.

FREE AT LAST

Victory over death
Thru Jesus Christ our Lord
Thru the flow of His sweet Blood,
Our soul will be restored.

There is no maybe, no, not one
There isn't any doubt
We can't hide away our sins
They're sure to find us out.

Death means nothing more
Than glory from the Throne
When my Lord is ready,
He will come take me home.

O death, where is thy sting?
The grave cannot hold me
Jesus set my spirit loose,
His blood has set me free!

WEEK THIRTY-SIX

LORD, I CAN'T WALK BY MYSELF

On our own, we could never keep God's commandments and live a holy and Godly life as we are told to do, according to *2 Peter 3:11 NIV*.

God knew that... He made us, remember? Adam and Eve sinned when they disobeyed God, and separated mankind from Him. But... God loved us so much; He still wanted a relationship with us. That's why He sent Jesus, His only Son, to earth. His death and the shedding of His precious, Blood, gave us peace with God again. The sin debt was paid in full by Jesus. We can now be "saved" from sin and death.

When Jesus returned to heaven to sit at the Father's right hand, He sent the Holy Spirit as our comfort and guide. After we repent of our sins and accept Jesus as our Lord and Savior, the Holy Spirit dwells within us, to help us.
It sounds easy, but, we are still human and God *still* knows that.
We need Jesus to hear our prayers and intercede for us with the Father.
We need God's mercy and compassion everyday... it's no coincidence... that's just how often His mercies are new...

"It is of the Lord's mercies that we are not consumed, because His compassions fail not. They are new every morning; great is Thy faithfulness." Lamentations 3:22-23 KJV

Thank You, O gracious and merciful God. Amen.

WE NEVER ARE APART

Mankind was lost forever
Buried deep in sin and shame
Then just like a shining light,
The blessed Savior came.

No matter who or where we are-
He's faithful to forgive
I'm so proud to know You Lord,
It's for You I want to live.

Only with Your help can I
Ever be so strong
I can't walk it by myself,
Please Jesus, come along.

Send Your Holy Spirit
To live deep within my heart
Let me know that You are there,
We never are apart.

WEEK THIRTY-SEVEN

LORD, I NEED YOUR HELP

As Christians, it seems we can put such a heavy burden on ourselves.

We try to be good, love one another, give to the poor, help everyone, go to church; put *enough* money in the offering; don't forget the missions!

And, that's just a short list of the things we try *to* do. The list is even longer of what we try *not* to do! When will we learn…? WE CAN'T DO IT!

"Come to me, all you who are weary and burdened, and I will give you rest. Take my yoke upon you and learn from me, for I am gentle and humble in heart, and you will find rest for your souls.
For my yoke is easy and my burden is light." Matthew 11:28-30 NIV

"God is our refuge and strength, an ever-present help in trouble." Psalm 46:1 NIV

MORE HELP:

Psalm 30:2 NIV…"O Lord, my God, I called to you for help, and you healed me."
Psalm 30:10 NIV…"Hear O Lord, be merciful to me; O Lord, be my help."
Psalm 30:11 NIV…"You turned my wailing into dancing; you removed my sack cloth and clothed me with joy,"
Psalm 30:12 NIV…"That my heart may sing to you and not be silent. O Lord my God, I will give you thanks forever."
Psalm 40:17 NIV…"You are my help and my deliverer."
Psalm 54:4 NIV…"Surely God is my help."
Psalm 63:7 NIV…"Because you are my help."
Psalm 70:5 NIV…"You are my help and my deliverer"
Psalm 121:1 NIV…"Where does my help come from?"
Psalm 121:2 NIV…"My help comes from the Lord, the Maker of heaven and earth."

Dear Father, we know this is a *short* list of Your help to us. Thank You for everything, especially for loving us. Amen.

TRYING IS TIRING

The power of God is an amazing thing
To a mortal such as I
Wonderful miracles He does produce
There's no need for Him to try.

I'm so weak in mortal form
I have no strength alone
And power... that without a doubt
Belongs to God alone.

Because He sent His Son
There's hope for even me
If He hadn't shed His precious Blood,
Where would salvation be?

Sing praise to my God above
Just glorify His Name
His strength and power He will share,
He loves us all the same.

Thru the presence of His spirit
Our joy and peace does lie
If we obey and trust His Word
We won't have to try.

For trying friend is not enough
To live as Christians do
Just ask God for His help
He will see you through.

Thank You Lord!
We always try so hard to do what's right.
We can't try hard enough.
Only with The Holy Spirit can we please God.
He lives in us and works through us.

WEEK THIRTY-EIGHT

GIFTS

This week is twofold, *"gifts and trials"*. I know I said the trials were in part two, and no, we aren't going back. But this is different... you'll see...

First read *Psalm 104* and meditate, just let the Lord speak to your heart.

"Praise the Lord, O my soul; O Lord, my God, you are very great, clothed with splendor and majesty." Psalm 104:1 NIV
If that were the contents of the entire Psalm, my mind could not comprehend the true meaning.

As I read on through to the end my heart is full of wonder and amazement. What a truly <u>AWESOME</u> God. My prayer will be:" I will sing praises to the Lord all my life; I will sing praises to my God as long as I will live. Amen

TRIALS

There have been so many times in my life, my heart was crushed and I felt I could not face one more day of disappointment. I'm sure everyone has had times like these... some more than others.

Just like there is no small "sin" with God, there is no small "broken heart."

The good news is:
There is no small "salvation", and there is no small "restoration."

He loves us all the same; we are all adopted children of the King.

He knows there is no small "hurt", but there is no small "healing."

Father, thank You for Your gifts of salvation, restoration, and healing. Amen

YOUR GIFTS

Thank You gracious Father
For the sun that warms my face,
For the wind that blows my hair,
For skies of blue,
For trees of green.
With these precious gifts of life
Nothing can compare.

MY TRIALS

Search my heart Dear Master, Friend
It is on You I can depend.
When troubles, trials, and storms befall
You are there Lord, thru it all.
Search me now Lord, find the flaw
Whichever sin Lord, large or small-
So that I may learn again.
Help me know there is an end
To trials and temptations great
I'm glad that it is not too late,
To trust in You and know Your Word
Bring back to mind the things I've heard
Help me, guide me, be my Light,
Lift me up and hold me tight.

WEEK THIRTY-NINE

THE PROMISE

With every ounce of imagination that I can muster, there is no way to explain the meeting of our Lord! Just try to fill in the blanks as you visualize the scene and scenery! Will we even remember what happened and how we got there, when we come before Him? If the Bible is given for our instructions for earth, while we are here, will we need it there?

Well, someday, we will have all the answers we need and our journey will have been worth the effort. What a great reward for simply loving the God who loves us; for willingly and lovingly, serving the King of Kings!

Remember what Paul wrote for instruction *"But we have this treasure in jars of clay to show that this all- surpassing power is from God and not from us. We are hard pressed on every side, but not crushed; perplexed but not in despair; persecuted, but not abandoned; struck down, but not destroyed." II Corinthians 4:7 NIV*
"Therefore we do not lose heart. Though outwardly we are wasting away, yet inwardly we are being renewed day by day.
For our light and momentary troubles are achieving for us eternal glory that far outweighs them all.
So we fix our eyes not on what is seen, but on what is unseen. For what is seen is temporary, but what is unseen is eternal." II Corinthians 4:16-18 NIV

Heavenly Father, give us strength and courage as you gave Paul and the others who were patiently enduring for the promise of the prize. Amen

SITTING AT YOUR FEET

I love to claim the promise
Of Your redeeming grace
Jesus I can hardly wait
To see Your shining face

I'll sit and ask You questions
I'll get The Word first hand.
About the prophet Moses
And the sacred promised land.

I get excited when I think
Of sitting there with You
All old doubts have flown away
I know Your Word is true.

WEEK FORTY

MY BENDED KNEES

God has always blessed me with many wonderful acquaintances and even lots of friends. I was told once that if you have just one true friend you are very lucky. Well, I don't believe in luck, but I do believe in blessings!

I have been blessed with more than my share of honest, caring and trustworthy friends. My Mother always said," In order to have friends, you first must be one." That impressed me, because her life was a living testimony of the truth in her words. I only pray that I will be as blessed.

In spite of the close relationships we share, everyone has a separate life;
The spouses, children, grandchildren, and even the "other" set of friends. A few times I have needed a shoulder to cry on, or maybe a reassuring, pat on the head and no one was home! Oh no! Who will share the sadness and the joys and thanksgiving with us when that happens?

Remember... *"A man that hath friends must shew himself friendly, and there is a friend that sticketh closer than a brother." Proverbs 18:24 KJV*

"But from everlasting to everlasting, the Lord's love is with those who fear him, and his righteousness with their children's children. With those who keep his covenant and remember to obey his precepts." Psalm 103:17-18 NIV

Dear Father, help us remember to come to You first. You are the "One" with all the right answers, Your ways are perfect. Thank You. Amen

MY CONSTANT COMFORT

When we come on bended knees
And kneel at The Throne,
We never have to stand and knock
To see if You are home.

You're always there to help us
And hear a prayer or plea,
Precious Lord, I praise Your name,
For always hearing me.

I'm so thankful, Mighty Friend
It is on You I can depend.
When my heart is crying out
There really isn't any doubt
That you will hear my humble prayer
Because Dear Lord, You're always there.

WEEK FORTY-ONE

OUR WITNESS

One of my biggest fears has always been, that I will not be a good example of God's goodness and salvation. The Apostle Paul wrote:
"We put no stumbling block in anyone's path, so that our ministry will not be discredited." II Corinthians 6:3 NIV

I can get in my frustrated state, *otherwise known as the flesh*, too quickly sometimes; usually, over injustice which I feel has been against me or some other person, powerless in our society. Afterward, I am always so disappointed in my actions and/or reactions.

This is where Satan, the accuser, steps in...
HE tells me," <u>EVERYONE SAW YOU!</u>"
He asks me, <u>"WHAT KIND OF CHRISTIAN ARE YOU?"</u>
He wants me to believe that all those people were *about* to be "saved"...
but now, they aren't going to ... because of me! ... It's my fault!

Then, I remember, I don't have that kind of power, and it's not about me anyway.

God knows my heart, He knows I'm sorry, but I tell him anyway!
I repent... He graciously forgives... I go on...
.

"As a father has compassion on his children, so the Lord has compassion on those who fear Him; for He knows how we are formed, he remembers that we are dust."
Psalm 103:13-14 NIV

Dear Father, thank You for Your mercy and grace. *Isaiah 12:2 NIV "Surely God is my salvation; I will trust and not be afraid..."* Amen

HE'S ALWAYS NEAR

Christ Jesus as I live today,
What will I do for You?
Will I bring honor to Your name
In things I say and do?

I'm thankful for everything
You've blessed us with each day.
You hold our lives in Your hands
In every single way.

When night falls and darkness comes
And my heart is gripped with fear,
I'll stop and remember
Our Blessed Savior's near.
Praise God!

WEEK FORTY-TWO

A SERVANT'S HEART

I've had some wonderful examples of Godly women in my life, my mother, Leona Lindsey, her mother, Rosa Levan, and our neighbor, Evelyn Thomas.
They all three had the gifts of *helps* and *hospitality* to name just a few.

They were all mighty prayer warriors and never hesitated to tell the story of Christ Jesus and His love for us.
They loved to serve!
Anytime there was sickness, death, a holiday… anytime someone was in need, they were there to pray, comfort and help in any way possible. Happiness was derived from giving, unselfishly to anyone in need. They have all been released from this earthly home and forever more they will be with the Lord.

What a legacy to leave behind; a gentle spirit, helping hands, loving humility and a servant's heart.

Father, help us strive to excel in kindness and love. May we be remembered for something so important? Amen

"How, then can they call on the one they have not believed in? And how can they believe in the one of whom they have not heard? And how can they hear without someone preaching to them? And how can they preach unless they are sent? As it is written, 'How beautiful are the feet of those who bring good news!'" Romans 10:14-15 NIV

MAY I HELP?

Give me Words by which to live
A loving heart to forgive
Helping hands and busy feet
A smile to welcome all I meet.

A stronger mind to think things thru
More confidence in things I do,
See me humble, meek and mild,
For I have come Lord, as a child.

Now Almighty God above
We come to You in joy and love.
Help us see Your Word so clear
And feel Your Mighty presence here.

Help us not to read, but LEARN
It's for Your filling we do yearn
Of the Holy Spirit, precious, sweet,
We're humbly yielded at Your feet.

WEEK FORTY-THREE

MY TESTIMONY

The first year of my walk with the Lord was quite a trip!
I had a lot of old friends... who no longer were!
I was quite a smoker in those days and that addiction was taken away from me when I prayed the sinner's prayer! I don't think my feet touched the ground for months! The whole world looked fresh and new!
My knees became red and sore from kneeling at my kitchen chair so long in the mornings. What an awesome and indescribable experience!

I read the Bible and prayed and God blessed my efforts over and over. Taking a day at a time was hard for me; I wanted to know <u>everything</u> now!
That's usually, not the way it works. It takes time to process and learn His ways. He knows how fast and how slow. It's like feeding a new baby its baby food with a spoon; little bits at a time, otherwise... we choke!
His ways are perfect... He is God!

"I have much more to say to you, more than you can now bear."
John 16:12 NIV

Dear Father, if Jesus was careful not to give the disciples more information than they could process...how much more are we in need of small portions for easy digestion and suitable application?
Thank You for caring for us so much. Amen

TRUSTING IN HIM

A year of walking in the faith
So quickly has gone by.
I've been so happy in The Lord,
The year has seemed to fly.

I've had problems, that's for sure
You've always helped me thru.
I have leaned upon Your arm,
I've gotten strength from You.

Each day at a time, You say,
Don't try to figure it out,
Don't give Satan another chance,
To fill your mind with doubt.

A new year we are starting now
On You I can depend
To always help me step by step,
Until the next year's end.

WEEK FORTY-FOUR

DAY BY DAY

Of all the people I would never have believed would have gone astray...
The last one would have been... Me!
All the obstacles Satan put in my way for four years, I made it through. Even when our son Gary was hit by a car at age five, I didn't blame God. As a matter of fact, I pressed in harder and prayed for strength. We prayed, God answered and we made it!

Shortly after I wrote this poem, maybe I was getting too self-assured.
A situation came up that I could not forget or forgive! I did blame God!
Where was He? Why did He allow this to happen, in our home? I was working for Him. I turned my back and walked away...
I thought things could not get worse, but they did and quickly!

God could have struck me dead, but He loved me even when I was unlovable. He allowed me to wander around in the wilderness until, I lost my pride and haughty attitude.
"'For I know the plans I have for you,' declares the Lord, 'plans to prosper you and not to harm you, plans to give you hope and a future.'" Jeremiah 29:11 NIV

When I came to the end of me and lifted my hand up to Him... His hand was already there, reaching down ready, willing and able, to pull me up. When I asked His forgiveness, He restored my soul and welcomed me as a lost sheep... back to the sheep shed.

"Surely the arm of the Lord is not too short to save, nor his ear too dull to hear."
 Isaiah 59:1 NIV

NOT BY MY MIGHT

I'll keep on keeping on Dear Lord.
I've known that from the start.
What the Holy Spirit tells me,
Help me hide it in my heart.

Oh sure, I get discouraged,
Surely, each and every day.
But the Holy Spirit leads me,
To find the time to pray.

Does it help? It surely does,
If you trust, He'll understand.
And up and out of darkness,
He will lead you by His Hand.

Will I give up? No! Never!
I'll not let Satan have his way.
For by the strength of God alone
He keeps me day by day.

WEEK FORTY-FIVE

NO REST, NO PEACE... ALONE

While I was away from the Lord...
The Holy Spirit convicted my heart all the time.
Many people would say conscience or co-incidence... not me!

I know that gentle tug, that soft whisper that says...
you know better than that!

You know the True and Living God... come back home.

There really is no place for a child of God... away from God.

You are a stranger in a strange land; parched in the desert.

Thank God... *"If we confess our sins, he is faithful and just to forgive us our sins, and cleanse us from all unrighteousness." 1 John 1:9 KJV*

"Set me as a seal upon Thine heart." Song of Songs 8:6 KJV

FULL CIRCLE

Dear Lord, I've gone full circle
Now, I do know how-
Your people sort of, drift away,
Forgetting every vow.

For I have been forgetful
And I've been neglectful too
My mind went back into the world,
And slowly hid my view.

Precious Holy Spirit
You've never left my side
Your often gentle tugging,
Proves, You still abide.

The mind is full of many things
Plus worries of the day
We must be very careful,
Or our heart starts to stray.

Lord I know, You saved my soul
You live within my heart,
Please restore my peace of mind
And heal the broken part.

WEEK FORTY-SIX

MY FRIEND... GOD'S SERVANT

I was driving down the old dirt road, nothing special on my mind
I saw my friend, I stopped to talk, today I had the time.

As I sat and talked to him,
I knew he worried for my soul.
Getting me to come to church was his final goal.

We talked of many, many things,
Of friends we both knew well
And how if you don't live for God
Your soul is bound for Hell;

The hatred in the hearts of men;
How friends must lead the way;
I wondered if somehow, he knew
That I had gone astray.

The days have grown so long
The months have soon passed by
It doesn't seem so long ago,
That I would sit and cry.

I had a burden for the souls
Of those that I hold dear
Now, my heart first thinks of... me
Now, I shed a different tear.

Oh, Lord my God, where did You go,
How could you ever be so far?
To me today, Your love is farther,
Than the farthest star!

But friend, my friend today you stopped
My thirsty soul did feed.
Today God used you once again,
To plant another seed!

"A word fitly spoken is like apples of gold in pictures of silver." Proverbs 25:11 KJV
Written for Jerry Good

WEEK FORTY-SEVEN

MY HEART

Hearing God's instruction clearly can be very difficult...
I would like to say it's easy and here's how you do it...
The fact is, I just don't wait well! This is the biggest problem!
It gives me hope to remember how the "Bible Greats" also had that problem.
How about Abraham and Sarah...? Read their journey in the book of *Genesis*.

If we could only remember that God has a plan ... **THE PLANS**... for us. *"'For I know the plans I have for you,' declares the Lord, 'plans to prosper you and not harm you, plans to give you hope and a future.'"* Jeremiah 29:11 NIV

The prophet Isaiah proclaimed, *"I will wait for the Lord, who is hiding his face from the house of Jacob. I will put my trust in him."* Isaiah 8:17 NIV

David did not hesitate to declare: *"In the morning, O Lord, you hear my voice; in the morning I lay my request before you and wait in expectation."* Psalm 5:3 NIV

If we read only the Psalms on this subject, we would stay busy. It is an interesting and helpful study too. Look at the sheer hope found in *Psalm 27:14 NIV*:
"Wait for the Lord; be strong and take heart and wait for the Lord."

Dear Lord, help us to seek your face, to let our heart be known, and to worship you in Spirit and in truth... and... help us wait well! Amen

HELP ME HEAR YOU

My heart is heavy
My spirit is light
My mind is soaring
As an eagle in flight.

So many decisions
And my thoughts in my brain
Some will bring pleasure
Some will bring pain.

Lord help me to handle
All that must be
Help me to know,
Is this You or just me?

WEEK FORTY-EIGHT

IT'S ABOUT HIM NOT ME

"And I looked but there was no one to help: I was amazed and appalled that there was no one to uphold truth and right." Isaiah 63:5 AMP

Along with my new position as supervisor came a new challenge, to live my "walk" of faith and love. It was not an easy task!

Word traveled fast that I was a Christian. Although I was ignored and even hated by some, for the most part... that was a good thing.

Part of my job was to walk the floor area helping and answering questions. It was a huge open area and I could see when anybody walked towards the restroom or the break room. I had to watch them because management was watching me! Then I had to follow-up and get them back to work! Many times I would find hurting women crying in the bathroom.

It soon became a daily event to pray with and for a co-worker experiencing marital problems, sick children, aged parents, or sickness. I felt honored to be used by the Lord. I thanked Him and prayed for His hand to guide us.

Management was very strict and quite unfair to most of the employees. It was stressful work for little pay. Everyone feared for their job at one time or another.

I was usually the strong encourager, but...

One day *my world* collapsed while at work, and I could not hide *my tears* as *I ran* toward the restroom. After I cried and gained composure, I suddenly realized... not one person had come to check on me! Of course, my feelings were hurt and I truly felt used and unappreciated for all the times I had gone to comfort others.

I thought they would have at least acknowledged *my pain*!

Later that night as I was trying to put it together, the Lord showed me the answer...

Fear of the enemy.

"Reproach hath broken my heart; and I am full of heaviness: and I looked for some to take pity, but there was none; and for comforters, but I found none." Psalm 69:20 KJV

FEAR OF THE ENEMY

When you came to me lonely
I was glad to be your friend.

When you came to me afraid and sad
I was happy to pray for you.

When you didn't know where to go-
You came to me and I was happy to be there

To hug, smile, and pray.

But...

Today I needed a friend – today
I looked around the room but found no one!

I needed comfort, hugs, and prayers too,

But...

I was all alone.

Then...

I realized how You must have felt, Dear Jesus,
Not that I compare myself to Your Majesty, Lord-

But...

You gave all, You love all.
Even Your chosen 12 let you down... even denied knowing You.

THEY FEARED THE ENEMY!

I could see why my friends didn't
Come to comfort me...

THEY FEARED THE ENEMY!

We all have many enemies:

Addictions, pain, depression, just to name a few.

We worry about losing friends, family, home, and safety.

On that job, I experienced much hurt and pain - Women and men who were homeless and lived in shelters.

Some were paroled prisoners who lived in a half-way house. One morning as I was driving to work, I saw a young man named Rob walking in the rain. I stopped and gave him a ride to work. He and a couple of other men had gone to church with me a few times. I knew he, like so many others, was struggling with such low wages. He trusted me and we talked that morning about his future. He was about to be released. He was afraid. That night he held a knife to the throat of a cashier and was arrested and put back in jail! What more could I have done to help?

One girl was beaten by her husband while another woman met a truck driver on the internet and took her two children to Oklahoma to live with him. We all pleaded with her not to go - but she did! We never saw her again.

Many didn't have enough food to eat or gasoline to get to work! Some were retired or disabled and couldn't live on their income, and the list goes on...

Yes, we have many enemies:

Anger, fear, poverty, hatred, and unconcern for others.

But... our ultimate enemy (of course) is Satan and sin. He loves tearing our lives apart and he laughs as he watches the hurtful drama unfold. How sad!

But... he is powerless when we turn to Jesus because...

"Greater is He that is in you, than he that is in the world."
1 John 4:4 KJV

WEEK FORTY-NINE

THE SONG

I'm moving on, I'm moving out
I'm getting stronger everyday
By the power of the Holy Ghost,
I'm on my way...

I thank Him in the the daytime
I thank Him in the night
By the power of the Holy Ghost,
He holds me tight.

Sing praises to the Son of Man
Sing praises of His birth
Rejoice in His Holy Name,
Have peace on earth.

THE DREAM

My pastor, Lois Hoshor, said "Some people say they are being beat to death by trials...

I tell you that you are being beaten to life by the Holy Ghost. He is dealing with you in ways you can't even imagine. Let go and let God. He knows your heart. He knows the rest of the story. Just praise him, be obedient, be faithful and true. Let God be true and every man be a liar. Praise Him, thank Him, glorify the sweet Name of our Lord and Savior, Jesus, and move on..."

I woke up singing The Song!

"But grow in grace, and in knowledge of our Lord and Savior, Jesus Christ. To Him be glory both now and forever. A-men'" II Peter 3:18 KJV

WEEK FIFTY

Deuteronomy 30:19 KJV – *"I call Heaven and earth to record this day against you, that I have set before you life and death, blessing and cursing: therefore choose life that both thou and thy seed may live."*

THE DAYS COME QUICK

EACH DAY'S TOO LONG,

AND I'M SO TIRED OF BEING STRONG.

TODAY I FEEL I WILL COLLAPSE…

BUT, WILL I?

I DON'T KNOW………..PERHAPS!

All the time I was in the desert, a hot and dry place, without leaning on the Lord, I still heard His voice, but I was too hurt and stubborn to repent and come 'back home.' I had not yet learned… there is no middle ground!

I lay my life out before you, hoping you will not fall into the same traps that I have.

If only one person will repent and come to God sooner and will learn that you can't get mad at God and win… HE IS GOD!

And they will not let Satan destroy a life and a family… then any pain or embarrassment that I feel will be worth it.

I was so wrong and I am so sorry!

Mae Kane – Lost 'Sheep' Found
1974-1982

Finding Faith –Learning - Growing
1983-1993

Wounded, Foolish, Sinful, 'Sheep', Mad at God – Left the Safe, Green Pastures – Wandered Around in the Wilderness – Lost and Alone!
1994-1997

Mae Kane-Jessup – Searching for the Path Home
1998-2005

Repentant 'Sheep' – Begged for Mercy and Forgiveness for my Sin and Shame – My Father was Waiting to Welcome me Back to the 'Sheep Shed', Where I Found Help for my Hurting Heart and New Hope for my Future
2005-

Mae McKnight – Thankful for my Husband, Home, and Family – Pursuing the Promise to Walk thru God's Plan for my Life

"'For I know the plans I have for you,' declares the Lord, 'plans to prosper you and not to harm you, plans to give you hope and a future.'"
Jeremiah 29:11

www.ingramcontent.com/pod-product-compliance
Lightning Source LLC
Chambersburg PA
CBHW071453040426
42444CB00008B/1318